MW01706812

Nursing Documentation

Reduce Your Risk of Liability

Patricia A. Duclos-Miller
MS, RN, CNA, BC

SECOND EDITION

hcPro

Nursing Documentation: Reduce Your Risk of Liability, Second Edition is published by HCPro, Inc.

 5 4 3 2 1

First edition published 2004. Second edition 2007.

ISBN 978-1-60146-035-6

HCPro, Inc., provides information resources for the healthcare industry.

Patricia A. Duclos-Miller, MS, RN, CNA, BC, Author
Rebecca Hendren, Managing Editor
Jamie Gisonde, Executive Editor
Emily Sheahan, Group Publisher
Stephanie Silverstein, Editorial Assistant
Darren Kelly, Books Production Supervisor
Liza Banks, Proofreader
Susan Darbyshire, Art Director
Janell Lukac, Layout Artist
Claire Cloutier, Production Manager
Jean St. Pierre, Director of Operations

Arrangements can be made for quantity discounts. For more information, contact:

HCPro, Inc.
P.O. Box 1168
Marblehead, MA 01945
Telephone: 800/650-6787 or 781/639-1872
Fax: 781/639-2982
E-mail: *customerservice@hcpro.com*

Visit HCPro at its World Wide Web sites:
www.hcpro.com* and *www.hcmarketplace.com

5/2007
21198

Contents

About the expert

Patricia A. Duclos-Miller, MS, RN, CNA, BC

Patricia A. Duclos-Miller, MS, RN, CNA, BC is currently a full-time associate professor in nursing at Capital Community College in Hartford, CT. In addition to this position, she is a senior consultant for the Kelsco Consulting Group in Cheshire, CT, a special lecturer for the University of Connecticut's management in nursing graduate program, and a per diem supervisor at Bristol Hospital, CT.

Duclos-Miller is a registered nurse, board certified by the American Nurses Credentialing Center (ANCC) in nursing administration. During her 33 years in nursing, she has been a director for quality improvement, director of nursing in acute, home health, and long-term care settings, and a staff nurse in the specialties of medical-surgical, mother-baby, and neonatal intensive care nursing. She is a recognized speaker on contemporary nursing topics, including quality improvement, team building, and documentation issues.

Duclos-Miller has served in key leadership positions for professional nursing organizations and is a contributor to the newsletter **Strategies for Nurse Managers,** published by HCPro, Inc. She is the author of *Stressed Out About Your First Year of Nursing,* the first and second editions of *Managing Documentation Risk: A Guide for Nurse Managers,* and the first and second editions of the handbook *Nursing Documentation: Reduce Your Risk of Liability,* published by HCPro, Inc.

Nursing Documentation

Reduce Your Risk of Liability

Intended audience

- Staff development educators
- Nurse managers
- Registered nurses (RNs)
- Licensed practical nurses (LPNs)

Learning objectives

Upon completion of this course, the learner will be able to:

- discuss the purpose of documentation
- describe the critical elements of nursing documentation
- identify six categories of nursing negligence
- identify the importance of understanding contemporary nursing standards and the contents of his or her state Nurse Practice Act
- list eight charting errors to avoid
- list three risk-management pointers that ensure a well-documented record
- list five tips for improving documentation that will reduce your liability risks

What is clinical documentation?

Clinical documentation in a patient's clinical record includes anything that relates to patient care during a visit, stay, or encounter. In the inpatient setting, some of the important pieces of documentation include the following:

Attending-physician documentation—In all patient-care settings, the attending physician bears the primary responsibility for documenting medical care in the patient's record. This is based on the requirements set by federal and state law and insurers. The attending physician provides the appropriate care based on the opinion of other healthcare providers and data that are in the clinical record.

Other physician documentation—Consultants, anesthesiologists, radiologists, cardiologists, and pathologists may contribute to the clinical record of a patient. Consultants contribute to the clinical picture of the patient and assist the attending in his or her plan of care. This can be found in consultative summaries, interpretation of diagnostic information, or physical exam findings.

Nursing documentation—One of the most critical components of the patient's medical record. The information the nurse documents is instrumental in noting what, in terms of patient care, occurred during the encounter, as well as in creating a picture of the patient's status during his or her care and status at discharge.

Other clinical provider documentation—In addition to nursing documentation, other ancillary clinical staff who treat the patient contribute to the overall clinical picture of the patient.

Reimbursement—The clinical record is also used for reimbursement through coding patient diagnoses (e.g., ICD-9), as well as identification of the procedures and related care given during the encounter. The clinical record is evaluated in all practice settings, acute care, outpatient, home care, and long-term care. The documentation by all clinicians found in the clinical record provides a basis for accurate and valid reimbursement by third-party payers.

The purpose of documentation

What is the purpose of documentation? The answer could be to:

- Demonstrate that care was given
- Prove to state and federal surveyors that staff are meeting the mandated regulations
- Assist in achieving Joint Commission accreditation (formerly known as the Joint Commission on Accreditation of Healthcare Organizations or JCAHO)
- Burden nurses with paperwork

Nurses always have questioned the value of documentation. But it is important to understand that documentation in the medical record is used for communicating and demonstrating contemporary quality nursing care and not to burden the nurse with meaningless paperwork. In the past, nurses have not focused on the important role their documentation plays in helping their organization meet regulatory requirements. However, now there are many reasons for accurate, complete, and timely documentation.

Ideally, contemporary nursing documentation not only meets the required elements of documentation for the organization, but also ensures accurate patient information for internal and external medical-record auditors. It's crucial to understand that documentation is the key to avoiding allegations of malpractice, substandard or poor nursing care, and denial of reimbursement.

Your potential liability risks

In today's lawsuit-laden society, nurses need to understand that the clinical record either can avert a potential lawsuit or provide credence to plaintiff allegations that the care provided was negligent. The clinical record is the only document that will demonstrate whether all of the care rendered by everyone on the healthcare team was at a standard level of care.

Understand that although documentation seems to be burdensome and a secondary priority, it will be your salvation if the patient/family believes the care did not meet expectations. This is especially true when a patient files or voices a complaint about his or her care or when there is an adverse medical event, such as a fall, medication error, or failed equipment.

Threat to licensure

A single complaint against a nurse can start an investigation of a nurse's practice. The complaint can be filed by a patient, colleague, physician, or hospital administrator. The Board of Nursing regulates the practice of nursing in each state. The board has a duty to investigate all allegations. If the investigation agrees with the complainant that the nurse poses a clear and immediate danger to the public's health and safety, it will take disciplinary action.

Pertinent medical records, human resource files, and copies of the organization's policies and procedures will all be reviewed. The Board of Nursing also may ask an independent nurse consultant to review your documentation to determine whether your actions were appropriate. Actions that the Board of Nursing could take include censure, a letter of reprimand, probation (time defined), suspension, or revocation of license.

Civil litigation

Patients have high expectations of their medical and nursing care. When we do not meet their expectations, anger can turn into allegations of negligence and professional negligence lawsuits. Malpractice cases that arise out of alleged nursing errors in hospitals are increasingly making local and national headlines. Individual nurses are now being named to avoid statutory caps on payments.

A negligence lawsuit typically is a civil case. The plaintiff relies on tort law, which includes professional negligence. A tort is a violation of some duty in which the law allows the injured party to seek damages. Negligence is defined as conduct that falls below the standard established by law for the protection of others against unreasonable risk of harm. It includes the concept of "foreseeability," in other words, that the harm that occurred could have been anticipated.

For a nurse to be found negligent, a patient must prove the following:

- **Duty:** The patient must show that the nurse had a duty to the patient

- **Breach of duty:** The patient must define what the appropriate standard of care is and that the nurse violated that standard
- **Causation or proximate cause:** The patient must prove that this breach of duty caused the patient's injury
- **Damages or injuries:** The patient must prove that there are damages as a result of the breach or as a result of the nurse's negligent actions

Six categories of nursing negligence

A study published in the *American Journal of Nursing* analyzed 350 lawsuit case summaries, and found six major categories of negligence. The lawsuits centered on nursing documentation that described negligent behavior in terms of "failure to, lack of, incomplete, ineffective, and improper." The six categories are failure to:

- Follow standards of care
- Use equipment responsibly
- Communicate
- Document the patient's progress, response to treatment, injury; pertinent nursing assessment; and physician orders
- Assess and monitor
- Act as a patient advocate

The role your documentation plays

How does documentation tie into civil litigation? The attorney will educate jurors as to the importance of documentation in the medical record. They will inform them of why timely and accurate documentation is important and reflects good patient care. Therefore, jurors will view good recordkeeping as an indicator of quality care and poor documentation as an indicator of poor care. Poor nursing documentation in addition to other factors will decrease the credibility of the nurse. Again, the nurse could maintain that the care was provided, but the jurors will rely on the evidence in the medical record.

Case Study 1

Documenting completely to avoid allegations of negligent care

Lab tests of a 46-year-old man with lupus polymyositis overlap syndrome with cutaneous disease revealed that the man had a severely reduced white blood cell count. An IV was started on admission but not documented in the record until the next morning. The patient was stabilized and discharged on the fourth day following admission. During the night shift before discharge, the man complained of pain at the site of his IV. The IV was moved to the other arm. There was no documentation of this. The patient continued to complain of pain at the former IV site on the day of discharge. Nurses advised the attending physician of the patient's complaints. The physician evaluated the site, described it as a cellulitis, and discharged the patient before identifying a definitive diagnosis. He placed the patient on prophylactic antibiotics.

Case Study 1 (cont.)

That evening, the man returned to the hospital with increasing pain, redness, swelling, and the development of ulcerations at the initial IV site. He was diagnosed with necrotizing fasciitis, a rapidly progressing infection process that cannot be controlled or contained by prophylactic antibiotics. The patient underwent emergency surgery to remove the infected tissue. The infection continued to progress, and his right arm required amputation. His condition continued to deteriorate, and he died approximately 24 hours later as a result of gram-negative bacteremia and septic shock.

Source: Adapted from a Nurses Service Organization, Case of the Month, February 2004.

Q

Can you identify the documentation missing from this situation that may be crucial in defending the organization from allegations of negligent care?

A

1. Documentation of the start of the IV. By not doing this, it caused subsequent nurses to fail to change the IV within 48–72 hours of its start.

2. A report of the patient's continued deterioration on the day of discharge.

3. A definitive diagnosis was not identified and recorded when the patient was discharged.

"Infusion therapy-related lawsuits are among the fastest-growing category of litigation brought against nurses" (Rosenthal 2005). Lawsuits can be filed for insertion, infiltration, and phlebitis issues.

Case Study 1 (cont.)

Your staff must document all aspects of their care with regard to IV care. There are established standards published by the Infusion Nurses Society and the Centers for Disease Control and Prevention. Be sure your policies, protocols, and documentation form include these standards. When looking at nursing documentation and developing an audit tool, remember that accurate, concise documentation is your best defense.

Look for nursing documentation that includes:

- IV insertion:
  - Date and time of insertion
  - Type, length, and gauge of the catheter inserted
  - Name of the vein used
  - Number and location of attempted insertions
  - Type of dressing used
  - Patient response to the procedure
  - Nurse's name and credentials
  - Solution that is infusing

- Continuous assessment:
  - Patient's tolerance of the IV therapy
  - Site appearance (use a standardized scale for this assessment)
  - Site care including dressing changes and equipment per protocol
  - Patient/family education
  - Discontinuation of the therapy
  - Any communication with other healthcare team professionals related to the IV device)

Reference: Rosenthal, K. 2005. "Documenting peripheral I.V. therapy". Nursing 2005 35(7): 28.

Contemporary nursing standards

Regardless of whether you have chosen to become a member of a professional nursing organization, the established and well-recognized standards written by an organization can be used as the official legal standard. *The Scope and Standards of Nursing Practice* was first published by the American Nurses Association (ANA) in 1973. These standards are used to describe general and specialty nursing practice competency. All professional nurses should become familiar with the ANA's professional nursing standards in addition to its standards of nursing practice. Every profession has established guidelines, standards, and recommendations that are used when questions are raised about a professional or act. Nursing is no exception.

Your state Nurse Practice Act

It is your responsibility to know your scope of practice in your respective state. Your state's Nurse Practice Act will define what is expected of you when providing nursing care, and it will also define what each nurse staffing type (e.g., RN, LPN) is responsible for in that state.

If a nurse does not understand or comply with his or her state Nurse Practice Act, he or she will be vulnerable to action against his or her professional license. The practice of contemporary nursing takes into account what is expected of nurses when delivering patient care. Copies of your state Nurse Practice Act are usually available at the state Board of Nursing and/or department of public health Web site.

The consequences of an incomplete medical record

Incomplete documentation in patient clinical records can cause your organization legal and settlement fees; it can cause you to lose your license; it contributes to inaccurate statistical databases, lost revenue/reimbursement, and results in poor patient care by other healthcare team members. That's why every organization should ensure accurate and complete clinical documentation—at any cost.

An incomplete medical record:

- Demonstrates that care was incomplete
- Contains gaps reflecting poor clinical care
- Demonstrates noncompliance with organizational policies
- Is used to support allegations of negligence
- Is used to support allegations of fraud

The following are potential repercussions of incomplete or inaccurate documentation:

- Researchers wouldn't be able to conduct patient-related studies
- Safe patient care is compromised
- Reimbursement/gross revenue is decreased
- Findings of fraud and abuse could lead to federal prosecution

Case Study 2

Failing to record and report change in condition

A female patient presented to the emergency room in a coma. She was readmitted to the hospital, but stayed in a coma until her death several days later. The medical examiner identified the cause of death as a subdural hematoma. The review of the clinical record found the following history: The decedent had previously suffered a stroke and was on Coumadin therapy. She had fallen at home and was admitted to the hospital several days previous to the emergency department visit. During the first hospitalization, the physician had prescribed Toradol and Phenergan. The nurse was to watch for changes in the decedent's physical condition. It was found through interviews that the nurse had not informed the physician of the decedent becoming lethargic, or changes in blood pressure, heart rate, and respirations. The physician discharged the patient home without knowing or seeing the change of condition in the medical record.

The plaintiff claimed that the hospital's staff failed to obtain copies of the decedent's coagulation studies, failed to investigate the history of Coumadin therapy, failed to order a CT scan, failed to report changes in physical condition, and failed to obtain a neurological consult.

Source: Adapted from a Nurses Service Organization, Legal Case Study, June 2005.

Case Study 2 (cont.)

Q

What missing information would be highlighted by a quality review? Why is this information so important?

A

When the quality reviewer turns to the nursing assessment and daily flow sheet, he or she is looking for documentation of any significant patient history prior to admission, medication history, and daily assessment findings. These qualifiers would indicate the potential physical problems that may present themselves during the hospitalization. If the nursing staff do not document changes in condition and communicate them to the physician the consequences can be devastating to all involved. This is an example of an incomplete medical record, poor communication between the healthcare team, and substandard level of patient care.

Eight common charting errors to avoid

Avoid the following eight pitfalls to ensuring proper documentation:

1. Failing to record pertinent health or drug information
2. Failing to record nursing actions
3. Failing to record that medications have been given
4. Recording on the wrong chart
5. Failing to document a discontinued medication
6. Failing to record drug reactions or changes in a patient's condition
7. Transcribing orders improperly or transcribing improper orders
8. Writing illegible or incomplete records

Risk management recommendations

To ensure a well-documented patient record, consider these risk-management guidelines:

Document all care given. This will be measured by your state's Nurse Practice Act and standards of professional nursing practice. It also is proof that care was given.
Document conversations with providers. Include highlights of the conversation, when the provider was notified, his or her response, instructions, and orders.
Document the nursing interventions that occurred before and after notifying the provider. If the chain of command was used, document who was contacted, the time of the call, the message communicated, and the response.
Always complete all forms/documentation tools.
Document all sponge counts (e.g., operating room, labor and delivery).
Document what instructions the patient was given, his or her understanding of the instructions, and any conversations with the patient/family.
Use only your facility's accepted methods for correcting chart errors in the medical record.
Do not document opinions.
Never blame another individual or department in the clinical record.

Top 20 tips for improving your documentation

Here are practical suggestions to improve your documentation, as well as rationale for why these tips are worthwhile.

1. **Write legibly.**
   The Joint Commission and other regulatory bodies now cite facilities if the medical record cannot be read. The reason is simple: Any illegible entry could be misconstrued and lead to an adverse medical event. Patient safety is their first and foremost concern.

2. **Date and time all entries.**
   Doing so accurately documents all nursing actions and patient responses. Do not block chart (e.g., 7A–7P). Dates and times accurately indicate the author's notations. It is defensible and prevents misinterpretation of events when reviewed by others.

3. **Every entry must be accounted for.**
   Sign your name and credentials for every entry, even if it is one line. Do not leave spaces between your documentation and your signature. This demonstrates which healthcare provider entered which notation.

4. **Do not leave any blank spaces.**
   Draw a line through any remaining space left on your signature line. This way, someone else cannot enter a statement before your signature. It is a way to prevent forgery.

5. **Use black, permanent ink for entries.**
Do not use colored pens, pencils, or felt-tip pens. They do not photocopy well and can be altered.

6. **Do not erase, obliterate, or "white out" any portion of the medical record.**
To properly correct errors, draw one line through, write "mistaken entry," then initial, time, and date the line and continue to document the correct information on the next available line. This eliminates the misinterpretation of a cover-up.

7. **Write factual entries.**
Do not give opinions, assumptions, or meaningless statements, (e.g., "Had a good day," "Was drunk and obnoxious"). In addition to being accurate and complete, your observations, interventions, and patient responses should be objective so your entries cannot be misinterpreted.

8. **Record entries as soon as possible after care is given.**
Never document before a procedure or medication is given. A timely entry assists the nurse in documenting events accurately, as the facts are fresh and it does not leave one open to questions of reliability.

9. **Review institution policies regularly and adhere to them when documenting in the medical record.** This demonstrates professional accountability and compliance with institution policies. This is key in your legal defense.

10. **Follow institutional policy when adding omitted information to an already existing entry.** For example, your policy might stipulate you write "late entry" or "addition to nursing note of Mo/Date/Yr and time." Remember to date and time the information being added. This demonstrates your compliance with professional standards of documentation.

11. **Use only abbreviations adopted by the hospital.** This further demonstrates adherence to institutional policy and does not allow for misinterpretation of the entry. It is now a requirement and demonstrates compliance with Joint Commission standards.

12. **Make sure every medical record page has the patient's correct name and other identifiers.** This eliminates mistaken identification and wrong entries/notations. It also assists in proving that the documentation belongs to the patient when the medical record is photocopied for reimbursement purposes, legal cases, and so on.

13. **Be thorough when recording contact with a physician, supervisor, or others (including other staff nurses).**
Include the following information:
    - The manner of communication
    - The names of those contacted
    - What was discussed
    - What response took place as a result of the contact
    - Any new orders
    - The care provided
    - The patient's response to the new orders and subsequent care provided

    This gives a historical and accurate accounting of the event, and it proves that you used the chain of command and were a patient advocate for quality care.

14. **Do not countersign any order, narcotics count, narrative entry, or other documentation unless you can attest to the accuracy of the information.** This prevents you from being associated with any potential for liability at a later date.

15. **Record all unusual incidents, such as a fall or other type of patient injury. An incident report is not enough.**
Notations should be factual and objective. Document what you observed, any relevant clinical or other data, interventions, and response to intervention. Do not write "incident report completed," as it makes the document accessible if the case goes to litigation.

16. **Always include an entry that reflects the time and condition of the patient when he or she leaves your care (e.g., for diagnostic work).**
This proves the patient's status while in your care and prior to leaving your care.

17. **Thoroughly record patient transfer information.**
Make sure you include:
    - Date and time of transfer
    - Patient condition when transferred
    - Who provided the transfer
    - Where and to whom the patient was transferred
    - Manner of transfer

This proves the patient's status while in your care and prior to the patient leaving your care.

18. **Always record consent for (or refusal of) treatment.**
    It can be a:
    - Written consent
    - Refusal form
    - Physician or RN documentation in progress notes

    Include critical discussion points to demonstrate that you discussed them and the level of patient/family understanding. This demonstrates informed consent.

19. **Include any patient/family teaching and discharge planning.**
    This withstands legal challenges to your professional standard of care. Ensure the completeness of documentation, accuracy, and the patient's/family's ability to understand instructions. Patient/family teaching is mandated by The Joint Commission and federal/state regulations.

20. **Record the disposition of any personal belongings of the patient (e.g., dentures, glasses, jewelry, or money).**
    This assists in the defense of accusations that belongings were lost when, in fact, they were sent home with the patient or family. Your organization may have a policy about this.

Some material in this handbook was adapted from the following sources:

Croke, E. 2003. "Nurses, negligence, and malpractice." *American Journal of Nursing* 103(9):54–64.

Greenwald, L. 2003. "Malpractice and the perinatal nurse." *Journal of Perinatal & Neonatal Nursing* 17(2):101–110.

Sheehan, J. 1997. "Safeguard your license: The disciplinary process." RN 60(1):53–56.

Showers, J. 2000. "What you need to know about negligent lawsuits." *Nursing 2000* 30(2):45–48.

Final Exam

1. **The purpose of nursing documentation is to:**
   a. Demonstrate that quality care was given
   b. Demonstrate compliance with The Joint Commission standards, as well as federal and state regulations
   c. Make more work for nurses
   d. Both a and b

2. **Threats to a nurse's licensure can be avoided by:**
   a. Following all contemporary nursing standards for your field of nursing
   b. Knowing your scope and responsibility based on your state Nurse Practice Act
   c. Documenting patient care based on the nursing process and organizational policies
   d. All of the above

3. **A single complaint against a nurse can start an investigation of his or her practice. Who can legally file a complaint against a nurse?**
   a. A patient
   b. A colleague
   c. A physician
   d. All of the above

4. Which of the following is a category of negligence that often leads to a malpractice lawsuit?

1. Failure to follow standards of care
2. Failure to communicate effectively
3. Failure to act as a patient advocate
4. Failure to medicate a patient

a. 1 and 2
b. 1 and 3
c. 1, 2, 3
d. All of the above

5. In court, a plaintiff's attorney will show the jury that timely and accurate documentation is important and reflects good patient care; poor documentation reflects poor patient care and decreases which of the following?

a. Time devoted to patient care
b. A nurse's credibility
c. Hospital revenue
d. Length of stay

6. Incomplete documentation can lead to many problems. Which of the following is not a problem of poor documentation?

a. Legal and settlement fees for your organization
b. Suspension or loss of your license
c. Poor patient care by other healthcare team members
d. A reprimand from the nurse manager

7. To avoid charting errors you must:

a. Record all pertinent health and drug information

b. Record all your nursing actions at the end of the shift

c. Record your opinion of the patient and family

d. All of the above

8. Which of the following is a good risk-management guideline for documenting nursing care?

a. Document all discussions and disagreements with other providers in your nursing notes.

b. Document the way you were taught in nursing school.

c. When the chain of command is used, document who was contacted, the time of the call, the message communicated, and the response.

d. If the lab did not contact you in a timely manner, be sure to blame it for the patient status worsening.

9. The abbreviations you use in a patient's medical record must be:

a. Easily understood by potential jurors

b. Exclusively those adopted by your facility

c. Written in blue ink

d. Spelled out at the end of the record

10. Frequent review of your organization's policies and procedures and adherence to them when documenting patient care demonstrates which of the following?

a. Professional accountability and compliance

b. Your abundance of on-duty free time

c. A lack of originality in your bedside techniques

d. None of the above

Answer key

1. d
2. d
3. d
4. c
5. b
6. d
7. a
8. c
9. b
10. a

Certificate of Completion

This is to certify that

____

has read and successfully passed the final exam of

Nursing Documentation Handbook

Robert Stuart
Senior Vice President/Chief Operating Officer